YOUR DIVINE COLORPRINT

THE COLOR CONTINUUM REVEALED

Written by Linda Kearney

Illustrated by Barbara Shackelford

Library of Congress Cataloging-in-Publication Data

Kearney, Linda

Your Divine Colorprint™: The Color Continuum Revealed

Copyright © 2020 Linda Kearney

All Rights Reserved.

Except for the inclusion of brief quotations in a review, no portion of this publication may be reproduced or utilized in any form or by any means without written permission from the publisher. This includes all mechanical, photographic, or electronic processes and copy or transmission for public or private use.

ISBN 978-1-7351207-0-6

1. Self-Improvement
2. Beauty, Personal

Publisher: Twelve Seasons Press

Printed in the United States of America

Designed by Wade Palmer

Contents

With Appreciation v

Introduction 1

Color and Your Appearance 5

    Power of Color 7

    The Energy of Color 10

    The Visible Spectrum 12

    Each Color in the Visible Spectrum Has Meaning 14

    The Color Continuum 24

    The Twelve Seasons on the Color Continuum 26

Personality Characteristics of the Twelve Seasons 29

    Bright Warm Spring 30

    Warm True Spring 30

    Light Warm Spring 31

    Light Cool Summer 32

    Cool True Summer 32

    Muted Cool Summer 33

    Muted Warm Autumn 34

    Warm True Autumn 34

    Dark Warm Autumn 35

    Dark Cool Winter 36

    Cool Clear Winter 37

    Bright Clear Winter 38

    Gifts and Talents 40

Face Shapes 43
    Round 43
    Square 44
    Inverted Triangle 45
    Rectangle 46
    Oblong 47
    Diamond 48
    Heart 49

Caring for Your Skin 51
    Skin Types 52
    Guide to Skin Care 54
    Skin Care Procedure 57

The Art of Makeup 65
    Makeup Brushes are the Artists Tools 68
    Cosmetics in your Seasonal Colors are the Artist's Palette 69
    General Guidelines for the Artful Application of Makeup 70
    Nail Care 89

Hair Fashion 91
    Animated and Lively Hairstyle 92
    Soft and Flowing Hairstyle 94
    Casual and Random Hairstyle 96
    Smooth and Defined Hairstyle 98

Conclusion 103

With Appreciation

To the pioneers of color analysis who opened my mind to the possibilities of color years ago.

To Barbara Shackelford for her shared love and passion for color, for her artistic eye and creativity, for her invaluable contribution to this book, and for our amazing friendship.

To Wade Palmer of Persudio Design whose knowledge and talent helped bring my vision to life and make this work a reality and for his efficient services in making my manuscript press-ready.

To Sharai McGill and Timothy Zaitzeff for editing this book.

To Michelle Parker for her support and assistance.

To my husband who always wanted me to do my best.

To my wonderful children and their extended families, whom I love dearly.

This book is for you.

Introduction

My introduction to color analysis was a life-changing event for me. Color analysis made such a noticeable change in those that chose to wear their seasonal colors in clothing and makeup that it was apparent that color analysis would be valuable in promoting my skin care and makeup business. It was my intent to learn the four-season color system that was popular at that time. Fortunately, Barbara Jacques, of the Academy of Color and Style of London, England, introduced me to the tonal theory of color analysis, which uses six seasons rather than four, during my training with her. That is the system of color analysis I used for years. The challenge was that some people seemed to need more and different shades or tones of colors than was to be found in any one of the six tonal seasons. In searching for answers as to why that was occurring, the writings of Suzanne Caygill, Kathryn Kalisz, and Bernice Kentner, pioneers in the industry of color analysis, led me to the conclusion that twelve is the correct number of color seasons.

Every person that has ever color analyzed me personally analyzed me as a Winter Season. I wore the colors of that season, adopted the persona of a person with Winter coloring, and lived as though Winter was my season for years. It was such a disservice. During all this time, I was aware that my favorite shade of red is a red orange which is not found in any

Winter color pallet. As I began using the twelve-season system, I sat in front of the mirror and draped myself in order to become familiar with the newly acquired drapes representing the twelve seasons. To my surprise, Winter was not my season at all. The drapes that complimented me most were those of a Bright Warm Spring. Those colors looked better than any of the Winter shades. The realization that my color season was incorrect caused me to re-evaluate and update my wardrobe, my hair style and my makeup to reflect my true color season. These changes made me feel more content, more aware of my own inner sense, and more confident. Others noticed and commented. The entire experience reinforced my conviction that there is power in knowing and using your seasonal colors as a lifelong guide.

By going through this process, it was obvious that most of the colors that work for a Bright Warm Spring were not to be found in any of the seasonal color palettes currently available. This led me to refine and update the work of the pioneers in the field of color and fashion and create my own system of color and style analysis. This required revising the color palettes to reflect the true colors of each season, designing the Color Continuum® to illustrate the Twelve Color Seasons and their relationship to one another, creating the Divine Colorprint™ which identifies the personal pattern which makes each person unique, and creating the Style Continuum for Women and the Style Continuum for Men--programs that describe, define, and determine the styles that work best for the season, the body silhouette, and the personality.

My business, FabYouLook, was reorganized and relaunched and a training program for FabYouLook® Stylists was instituted.

This book about color and another book (yet to be written) about style also resulted from my experience.

There is no way to put a price on the self-assurance and personal confidence that comes with knowing how to use color and style and having some skills to help you look and feel your best in every situation. Hopefully, the concepts shared within the pages of this book will help you understand more fully your own personal individuality and the impact color has on your life and in your own personal space.

Color and Your Appearance

Color has always been important to us. Color makes life exciting, interesting, and happy. Color has the ability to create or convey mood, perspective, shape, and harmony. Color is used to create beautiful images. People have a natural appreciation for color and its harmonies. They often like what they see instinctively, without always knowing why. This applies to art, architecture, interior design, clothing and makeup. Color is dynamic—always changing to communicate the seasons. Some people are drawn to the stark, clear, colors of winter, others to the unfolding of color that spring brings. Some prefer the soft colors of summer, and others the rich, earthy tones of autumn. Every person has a distinct color palette of colors they intuitively prefer.

The natural coloration of your skin harmonizes with your eyes, hair, features, and personality. When you add complimentary colors next to your skin, those colors reflect from your skin and enhance your appearance. The incorrect colors are absorbed into the skin and make you look dull and uninteresting. When colors are observed side by side, they influence one another. You are born with a complexion that reflects light and color based on the colors placed adjacent to those skin tones. Color Analysis is the method used to determine the shades and tones that harmonize with the undertone, intensity, and clarity of one's skin.

Color affects the way you feel about yourself and everything around you. Wearing the right colors for you will reflect your true, authentic self and personal energy. Your most reflective colors will lift your spirits and make you happy. Those colors will be invigorating and encourage creativity.

Power of Color

My experience doing Color Analysis has shown that colors that are complimentary will help you look thinner and younger. Lines and wrinkles will diminish or disappear. Your skin will look clearer. Teeth will look whiter. Hair will shine. Eyes will sparkle. In your proper colors, you will look and feel healthy, vibrant, defined, and confident. Wardrobe planning and getting dressed every day will be simpler. You will be able to shop with confidence. Knowing your colors will help in determining décor for your home and office that will enable you to be happy and productive. Surrounding yourself with supportive colors will help heal emotional trauma.

Others will trust you and pay more attention to your opinions when you wear your seasonal colors. They will perceive you as being well informed and knowledgeable. They will look to you for council and advice and see you as an authority figure.

Appearance counts every day and under every circumstance from the classroom to the boardroom and any place in between. Whatever you do in life, how you present yourself is important to your self-esteem and your success. According to the Institute for Color Research (CCI Color), people make a subconscious judgment about a person "within 90 seconds of initial viewing and that between 62% and 90% of that assessment is based on color alone."[1] You have 90 seconds to make a first impression. Others make some powerful assumptions within those few seconds. Your hair, clothing, and grooming habits have been thoroughly assessed. Your socioeconomic level, education level, and intelligence have been determined. Your personal potential, moral character, and trustworthiness have all been evaluated. Others have already decided whether you are worthy of their further attention. Unfortunately, once those decisions are made, those impressions last out of proportion to the time it takes for them to be formed. That is why you never get a second chance to make a first impression.

Whether this is fair or unfair does not change the fact that it is part of human nature and happens all the time in both the social and the business world. You can deny its existence and even believe that you are above this superficial behavior, but the truth is everyone does it automatically and subconsciously.

---

1 Jill Morton, "Why Color Matters," Colorcom, 2019, https://www.colorcom.com/research/why-color-matters.

You even do it to yourself. On days you do not leave the house, you will see yourself reflected in mirrors, windows, and doors approximately fifty-five times and will feel good about yourself or bad about yourself based on the way you look. Your self-talk about what you see always has a powerful influence on your self-esteem and performance.

You talk to yourself and to the world by how you present yourself. Every choice you make that concerns your appearance makes a statement that announces to the world who you are. You want to make certain that your message is: "Look at me, recognize me for who I am and for what I can contribute."

You are one of a kind. There is no one in the entire world exactly like you. You have a unique combination of features and characteristics that form a distinctive pattern that belongs to you alone. This pattern is your Divine Colorprint®. Your color season is the foundation of your Divine Colorprint®. Your seasonal colors create harmony and balance between who you are on the inside and how you appear on the outside. Everything about you relates to your color season. Factors such as personality, facial features, and hair are all related to your season. In addition, the silhouette of your body and your fashion preferences are an integral piece of your Divine Colorprint®.

The Energy of Color

Color is energy. It is not static. Color is vital and dynamic. Every person emanates color with a personal force field of energy. Color is a vibration of light and manifests itself in neuromagnetic wavelengths. Experts in the field of color theory have determined that colors have energy. Johannes Itten, a well-known Swiss painter whose research with color contributed to the creation of seasonal color analysis, said, "Colors are forces, radiant energies that affect us positively or negatively, whether we are aware of it or not."[2] Dr. Donald H. Andrews, professor emeritus of chemistry at John Hopkins University, stated:

The more man looks into the atom, the more he sees a power that is less and less material. The atom is essentially composed of waves, the significance of which lies in the harmonic relationships of their frequencies. Thus, we are concluding that the universe is not matter. It is number. It is music.

Pythagoras knew this over two thousand years ago. Today, we are returning to this concept.

But even more than this is the fact that the biological cell is giving us the clue to our biological inheritance. In every cell of the human body is light and **color** beyond the human spectrum, beyond imagination. There is movement too, as **light** streams into the cell from outside the body and from every other part of the body; and as **light** goes out from the cell into the body and beyond the body.

Here in the cell is the nucleus, wherein lies the mystery of life. Here our eternal name is written, vibrating with a harmony that will never cease.

Thus, we are transmitting **waves of color** and vibration to everyone around us—waves of

---

[2] Johannes Itten, The Elements of Color, (New York: John Wiley & Sons, 1970), 12.

thought and waves of action written in a veritable book of life.

This is where we live beyond time and space. Here we are projecting ourselves into the eternal and are growing in terms of **harmony and color** beyond imagination. ***Our destiny lies in this harmony***, in this infinitude, in this unity of life.[3]

Color harmony is one objective of a personal color analysis. Besides creating color harmony, a personal color analysis will visibly demonstrate how using color correctly for your season makes a significant difference in the way you look and also in the way you feel about yourself. A color analysis is also the basis for determining your Divine Colorprint™.

The Color Continuum® has as its inspiration the seven colors of the rainbow and the visible spectrum. Each of the seasons has a version of the colors on the visible spectrum, including orange.

Light, movement, waves, vibration, frequencies, energy, harmony—all those terms are used to characterize color. The objective of a color analysis and discovering your own Divine Colorprint® is to capitalize on the impact and power that color possesses for you personally.

---

[3] Bold and italics added.

The Visible Spectrum

It was Sir Isaac Newton that demonstrated that color is a quality of light. The visible spectrum is the light or the color that can be seen with the human eye. The visible spectrum consists of the seven colors of the rainbow. Each color in the visible spectrum has its own vibrating pattern of electromagnetic energy as illustrated below. The colors of the rainbow always appear in the same order: red, orange, yellow, green, blue, indigo, and purple.

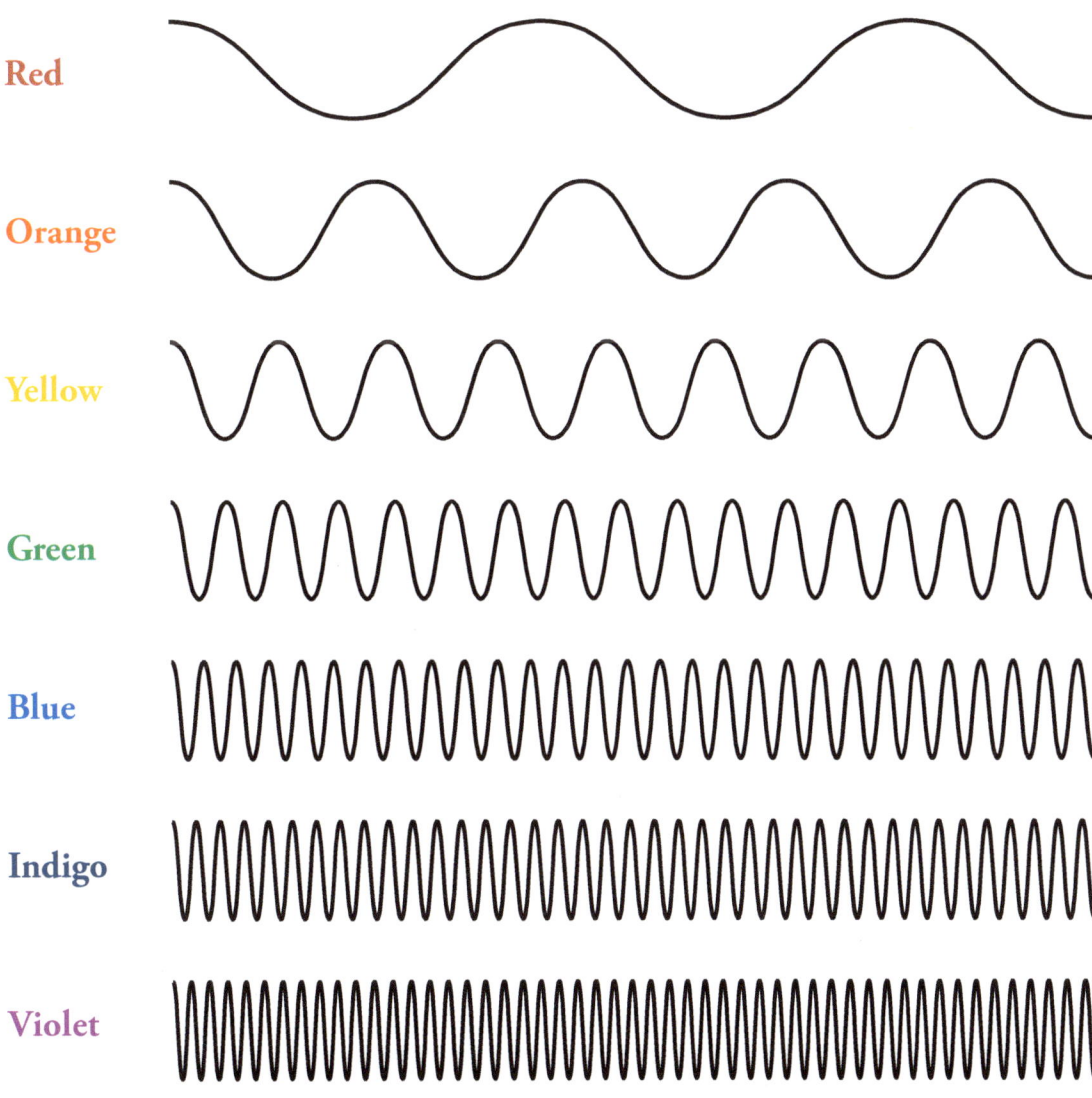

[4] Sources for many of the facts about the various colors include the following. Faber Birren, Color Psychology and Color Therapy, (Secaucus: The Citadel Press, Secaucus, 1950). Johannes Itten, The Elements of Color, (New York: John Wiley & Sons, 1970), 12. Wassily Kandinsky, The Art of Spiritual Harmony, (London: Constable & Co., London, 1914).

Each Color in the Visible Spectrum has Meaning

Red

- Red is a very intense color. Red demands our attention.

- Red energizes us and motivates us to action. It represents vitality and sensuality.

- Red warns of danger.

- We associate red with energy, strength, power, and determination.

- Red is the color of physical movement and awakens our life force. We associate red with our hearts and with love.

- Bright red has very high visibility. Red brings text and images to the foreground. It is often used as an accent color to encourage people to make quick decisions.

- Pink, one of the lighter shades of red, signifies love, romance, sensitivity, femininity, and friendship.

- Peach and salmon are variations of red that express youth and lightheartedness.

- Corals express health and renewal.

- The darker shades of red, such as burgundy or maroon, create an impression of dignity and maturity and are associated with leadership, courage, willpower, and vigor.

- The red browns suggest stability and are associated with the fall harvest. In heraldry, red is used to indicate courage.

Orange

- Orange is full of vitality. It is friendly and inviting, optimistic and uplifting.

- It is cheerful, creative, unique, social, flamboyant, adventurous, trendy, and motivating.

- Orange invokes spontaneity. It helps us overcome disappointments and sadness.

- Orange produces an invigorating effect on our brain and stimulates mental activity.

- As a citrus color, orange is associated with healthy food.

- Orange is the color of fall and an expression of the harvest.

- Shades of peach encourage communication, conversation, and good manners.

- The deeper shades of orange promote feelings of confidence, purpose, and ambition.

- Gold, which falls in the orange category, evokes the feeling of prestige.

- Gold symbolizes wealth, high quality, and wisdom.

- In heraldry, orange is symbolic of strength and endurance.

Yellow

- Yellow is the color of sunshine. Yellow is optimistic, uplifting, cheerful, and fun. It implies liveliness, happiness, joy, confidence, and enthusiasm for life.

- Yellow stimulates the intellect. It helps one to focus, study, and remember information. It is useful when making decisions.

- Yellow inspires original thought and inquisitiveness. It opens our minds to new thoughts and ideas and helps us create new ways of doing things.

- Yellow encourages conversation. It is a friendly color.

- Yellow promotes optimism, physical energy, and a sense of spontaneity.

- Light yellow expresses the awakening of the mind, making it open and alert.

- Lemon yellow is associated with intelligence, fresh ideas, and a joyous outlook.

- Golden yellow is the color of intense curiosity, intense interest, and intense focus.

- In heraldry, yellow indicates honor and loyalty.

Green

- Green is associated with nature.
- Green is an indication of new growth and vitality.
- Green is the color of renewal and restoration.
- Green is a hopeful color that allows us to anticipate things to come.
- Green revitalizes us when we are physically, mentally, or emotionally exhausted. It is a nurturing color for everyone.
- Green is a friendly color.
- Green is the color of prosperity and abundance, of finance and material wealth. It relates to the business world, particularly the financial world and banking.
- Pale green indicates new growth on plants. That shade of green represents new perspectives and new beginnings.
- Emerald green suggests abundance, wealth, and material well-being.
- Jade green indicates a generosity of spirit.
- Lime green creates a feeling of anticipation.
- Olive green is the traditional color of peace.
- In heraldry, green indicates growth, abundance, and hope.

Blue

- Blue is the color of the sky and water.
- Blue is associated with wisdom and intelligence.
- It symbolizes trust, responsibility, honesty, loyalty, and stability.
- Blue is considered beneficial to the mind and body. It slows human metabolism and reduces stress. Blue produces a peaceful, quiet, relaxing effect. It is strongly associated with tranquility and calmness.
- Blue is highly accepted among males. Dark blue is associated with depth, expertise, reliability, and stability. It represents order and direction in life.
- Blue is safe, predictable, and non-threatening. It demonstrates caring and concern.
- Pale blue inspires creativity and a sense of freedom.
- Sky blue is associated with health, healing, tranquility, understanding, and softness.

- Azure blue inspires contentment and a sense of purpose. Azure promotes a feeling of determination and ambition to achieve great things.

- Rich, saturated blues suggest authority and power.

- Dark blue represents knowledge, credibility, confidence, integrity, and seriousness and is the preferred color for corporate America.

- In heraldry, blue is used to symbolize a spiritual perspective and religious devotion.

Indigo

- Indigo is a deep midnight blue. The color indigo conveys a sense of drama.

- Indigo allows for deep concentration during times of introspection.

- Indigo conveys integrity, deep sincerity, and devotion to truth.

- Indigo loves rules and regulations, rituals and traditions and likes to follow things that have worked in the past and not move into unchartered territory.

- In heraldry, indigo represents intuition and perception.

Violet

- Violet has the highest vibration of energy in the rainbow or visible light spectrum.

- Violet represents imagination, dreams, and the future.

- Violet promotes introspection and spirituality.

- Violet encourages sensitivity and compassion.

- Violet encourages creative pursuits. Artists are often drawn to include violet in their work because it is unconventional, original, and unique and sets their work apart as being inventive, unusual, and individual.

- Violet contributes to peace of mind.

- Violet exudes a quiet, modest form of dignity, which is often appealing to others.

- Light purple or lavender is often associated with beautiful and glamourous things.

- The darker shades of violet, specifically purple, denotes sophistication and a trustworthy nature.

- Purple symbolizes dignity, luxury, wealth, power, and extravagance. Originally, only royalty, nobility, or the very rich could afford anything purple.

- In heraldry, purple represents righteousness and royalty.

White

- White light contains all wavelengths of visible light and is not considered to be a color.

- White represents purity and perfection. In heraldry, white represents peace and innocence.

Black

- Black is the total absence of light and is not considered to be a color. Black has no electromagnetic energy whatsoever.

- Black is only found in the color pallets of the three Winter seasons. For all other seasons, black drains their energy.

- Just a note—black does not make everyone look thin. Wearing the colors of your own season is the best way to flatter your figure.

- Black is associated with fear, hiding, death, and mourning. Often when people wear black and it is not in their season, they are hiding in some manner.

- In heraldry, black is the symbol of sadness and grief.

The Color Continuum

Four Characteristics of Color

1. **Hue:** The name we call a color or shade such as red, orange, or purple.

2. **Undertone:** Warm undertones have a yellow cast. Cool undertones have blue.

3. **Intensity:** Cool undertones have a blue cast. Light colors are pale or whiteish. Dark colors are intense or saturated.

4. **Clarity:** "Bright" denotes vivid or brilliant. "Muted" means soft and subdued.

Your skin is either **warm** or **cool**. It is **light** or **dark**. It is **bright** or **muted**. There are twelve combinations of these characteristics that create the Twelve Color Seasons on the Color Continuum®.

COLOR CONTINUUM®

The Twelve Seasons on the Color Continuum

The Color Continuum® is a visual illustration of the Twelve Seasons. There are no "neutral" seasons or combinations of seasons. Each of the Twelve Color Seasons has its own palette of colors. Each of those seasons is distinct and different from every other season. They all have equal value. The Color Continuum indicates that we may be closer to one of the adjacent seasons in our coloring and attributes than we are to another. Each season has variations of the seven colors of the rainbow. A shade of orange exists in the color palette for each one of the Twelve Seasons. The various hues in the color palette of any given season do not all match. Every color in one seasonal palette will work in combination with some of the other colors in that same palette but not all of them.

1. **Bright Warm Spring:** The most dominant characteristic of this seasonal color palette is brightness. Warmth is the secondary characteristic of this season.

2. **Warm True Spring:** Warm undertones are unmistakable as the dominant characteristic of this season. The golden undertones are the shades of sunshine or daffodils. The colors of Warm True Spring are warm, light, and lively.

3. **Light Warm Spring:** Light is the defining characteristic of this season. The light colors are accompanied with visible warmth.

4. **Light Cool Summer:** Light and fair with cool undertones are expressive of Light Cool Summer. Shine and shimmer are noticeably present in the color choices of this season.

5. **Cool True Summer:** Cool undertones are the outstanding feature that defines Cool True Summer.

6. **Muted Cool Summer:** Softness or gentleness of coloring is very evident in Muted Cool Summer. Grayed is descriptive of these muted shades.

7. **Muted Warm Autumn:** Soft and warm describe the colors of a person with the coloring of a Muted Warm Autumn.

8. **Warm True Autumn:** Warmth is evident as the dominant characteristic of this season. The undertones are rich and vibrant, as if from gold dust.

9. **Dark Warm Autumn:** Darkness will overshadow the warmth of this season. Nevertheless, warm undertones are easily detected and very distinctive.

10. **Dark Cool Winter:** One dark feature—usually hair or eyes—will be a determining factor in analyzing this season. Many—but not all—colors and shades of this season are very deep and rich.

11. **Cool Clear Winter:** Cool, clear colors and high contrast are indicative of the Cool Clear Winter. Their colors are pure and free from any cloudiness.

12. **Bright Clear Winter:** The striking intensity and bright luminosity of the Bright Clear colors of this season are immediately apparent. No other season can wear these colors without being totally overwhelmed by their strength.

Personality Characteristics of the Twelve Seasons

Each of nature's Twelve Color Seasons has certain character traits that are typical of that season. Knowing your special qualities will help you make the most of them. This will not only benefit you, but others as well. The differences in personalities within the Twelve Seasons are important to one another. Working together with the strengths of each Season allows for the accomplishment of great things. Springs move fast; Summers work at a slower, more deliberate pace; Autumns move in a determined way; and Winters move in a stately manner. Spring Seasons are full of ideas. Summers Seasons are very detail oriented and always need to work out the details before they begin a project. Autumns include people whose focus is on getting the job done. Winters are always seeking to improve and perfect the details or the process.

Characteristics refer to the distinctive qualities and behaviors that represent one's personal identity. These characteristics are present at birth and remain for a lifetime. Each Season has its own sense—its own special capacity for perception.

Bright Warm Spring

Bright Warm Spring people are very observant. They have the ability to see and assess what needs to be done in any given situation. Those whose season is Bright Warm Spring are full of ideas. New ideas will come before the first project or idea is brought to completion. They think fast. They make decisions quickly. They think fast, make decisions quickly, and bounce from one idea to the other at high speed.

Bright Warm Springs are very talkative and make great speakers. They thrive in professions that involve speaking in front of groups and training others. This season likes to tell stories to get their point across. They are great promoters and can motivate others to action. They excel in sales and anything that involves people skills. Bright Warm Springs do not like routine and repetition.

Warm True Spring

Warm True Springs are outgoing, friendly, and fun to be around. They like social gatherings and like to see that everyone is happy. Warm True Springs are naturally generous with their time and their money.

The ability to work on and accomplish many tasks at the same time comes naturally to them. Their thinking processes are quick and rapid and may appear random to others. They are also open and accepting of the thoughts and ideas of others. Warm True Springs are flexible and adapt easily to change. They are impulsive, may speak without thinking, talk too much, or exaggerate.

Light Warm Spring

Light Warm Springs are fun-loving and playful. They have a generally happy disposition. This Spring type is eternally ageless and young in spirit.

They have a natural ability to communicate well with people. They are empathetic listeners. Public relations or communications are a good fit for them as a job choice.

Light Warm Springs love people and love to help others. They will seek out ways to be helpful to their friends, family, and acquaintances. The person who is a Light Warm Spring is particularly sympathetic to small children and animals. They enjoy large family gatherings and events such as the circus, picnics, and dances. Entertaining for them comes naturally and is effortless and usually informal.

Goal setting come natural to a Light Warm Spring. Risk taking is another characteristic of this season. Light Warm Springs are energized by interruptions. They like a frequent change of pace in whatever they are doing. Light Warm Springs will daydream.

Light Cool Summer

Light Cool Summers have warm, loving natures. They possess the ability to see the relationship between many bits of data they collect. This season has the unique skill to gather the facts, classify them into categories, and then see the relationship between seemingly unrelated elements. Basically, they possess the ability to see the big picture.

The doing part of any project for some Light Cool Summers is slow because they are unrushed by their nature. Light Cool Summers are precise, methodical, and pay meticulous attention to detail. The Light Cool Summer does not like to see a task uncompleted.

Light Cool Summers needs time alone for reflection. They enjoy the outdoors—gardening is preferred over sporting activities. Another characteristic of this season is that they would rather play a supporting role than take the lead. When they are excited, the voices of Light Cool Summers rise in pitch, and they speak faster than is usual for them.

Cool True Summer

Cool True Summers do not like to be rushed. They like time to get used to new ideas. Cool True Summers are extremely committed to completing any task or project. They are reliable.

People of this Season like to teach and give instructions. They excel in situations where a mediator, mentor, or counselor is needed.

They donate their time for the benefit of others and try to contribute to society at large. They are nurturing by nature and make wonderful nurses.

Cool True Summers have iron wills. Once they make up their mind about something, they are unchangeable. They like comfortable and stable situations. This season loves the comfort of home and to be surrounded by their family and friends.

Cool True Summers emotions are always close to the surface. Their feelings are easily hurt and they cry readily.

Muted Cool Summer

Muted Cool Summers are adaptable and dependable. They believe in their ability to be successful under any circumstances. This season recognizes the value of goal setting. They work through projects at a determined pace.

Those who are of this season are very stubborn. They expect others to meet their expectations. Muted Cool Summers are not inclined to raise their voice, speak their mind, or display anger outwardly but instead will give you the silent treatment when they are displeased.

Muted Warm Autumn

Muted Warm Autumns are disciplined and comfortable when they feel they are in control. This particular Autumn season is very thoughtful about the decisions they make. They think they know what is right and good for themselves and for everyone around them and expect others to do what they suggest.

This Muted Warm Autumn Season is strong willed and usually get their own way They like to work from a plan and do not adjust to changes in that plan easily. Change of any kind does not come easy for Muted Warm Autumns. They are extremely capable and are often put in charge of projects.

Warm True Autumn

Those whose season is Warm True Autumn are action- and results-oriented. They like to make things happen. They are very decisive. They easily handle many tasks at once and always finish what they start. When they are on task, their focus becomes extremely narrow, and they are not capable of noticing what goes on around them. They are abrupt and to the point and may offend others. Their focus is on the objective—not on the people.

Warm True Autumns are authoritative, strong-willed, and confident. This Autumn Season will figure out what needs to be done and will want to do it themselves. Warm True Autumns have high expectations for themselves and for others. They value achievement. They strive for excellence. They are bored by trivia and small talk.

Warm True Autumns have a strong personality and are leaders by nature. They are often entrepreneurs because they want to be their own boss. Women who are the Warm True Autumn Season will look for an outlet for their driving energy. They are often the PTA president, the sports moms, the volunteers. True Autumns like the outdoors and are often involved in sports that allow them to be out in nature.

Dark Warm Autumn

Dark Warm Autumn people have a lot of personal drive. They are hard workers and like to keep busy. They like a challenge. You can count on them to do any job assigned to them in an effective manner.

Dark Warm Autumns are true to a cause. They have a low tolerance for mistakes and feel a need to correct wrongs. They take charge in group situations. They are caretakers by nature. Dark Warm Autumns are self sacrificing and generous with their time and energy. Time alone is essential for them to regroup.

Dark Cool Winter

Dark Cool Winters are authoritative and purposeful. They are people of great determination and willpower. They are tenacious and work with great resolve. When Dark Cool Winters are on task, they are difficult to distract.

Dark Cool Winters are attracted to confident leaders. They will not follow anyone who does not exude confidence. Their mantra is "lead, follow, or get out of the way." This season will assume responsibility and take the lead when working on a project.

The Dark Cool Winter wants to do the right thing and follow the rules. They value honesty. They are prone to want things done their way because they have carefully considered all options, and it only makes sense to them to do it the way they have concluded is best. This season has no patience with indecision. Once a plan is in place, they do not like any changes to the plan.

They are loyal friends and often maintain friendships throughout their life. They have high expectations of themselves and everyone around them. They strive for perfection and expect the same from others.

Cool Clear Winter

Cool Clear Winters are attention getters. Their appearance is dramatic and impressive. In clothing, they have little need for ornamentation. Cool Clear Winters are naturally drawn to gracious living. They love to be surrounded with luxurious and beautiful things.

Cool Clear Winters walk with little movement in their limbs and body and with a very straight posture. They are naturally erect, poised, and still.

Cool Clear Winters like order both at home and at work. They find great comfort in routine. They excel at tasks that require concentration and repetition. Cool Clear Winters are precise, accurate, detailed, orderly, and prone to genius. They like facts, figures, graphs, and charts. They like balance and symmetry. They have an innate sense of design.

Those who are of this season are persistent and unhurried. They work best when given one task to complete at a time. They like specific instructions. They find interruptions and distractions extremely frustrating. The Cool Clear Winter person needs time to think and time to do their assigned project. They need to be able to get themselves organized and break down whatever they are doing into manageable tasks. They may also have difficulty stopping what they are doing if the task is unfinished no matter what the circumstances.

They like to follow traditions and keep the rules. This season typically remembers special days and dates, such as birthdays and anniversaries.

The Cool Clear Winter is not naturally talkative, so when they speak, others tend to pay attention to what they have to say. They do not like to be interrupted while speaking. They like others to respect their space.

Bright Clear Winter

Bright Clear Winters are dramatic and distinctive. No other season can wear the high color saturation that is so complimentary to the skin tones of Bright Clear Winters.

This is the Season that will wear makeup and dress up every day. It does not matter if they are home alone or out in public.

Bright Clear Winters like to be the center of attention and are often found in theater, movies, radio, or TV. They may be authors of books or composers of music. They usually like to perform for others and may have a large following of admirers.

Sales is an area where Bright Clear Winters do well, but only if it is not high-pressure sales and people come to them for their products or services.

Knowing the personality characteristics associated with each of the Twelve Seasons leads to understanding, accepting, and appreciating everything about yourself and every other person in your circle of influence.

In addition to the personality traits characteristic of their Season, each person will have traits that are found in other seasons as well and will also have their own special gifts and talents.

Gifts and Talents

Gifts are special abilities, capacities, or natural endowments bestowed on recipients and are acquired without effort on their part and without being earned. To be of value, gifts must be recognized and developed.

Talents are acquired skills or achievements that require effort, focus, and energy from the individual.

- Gifts and talents in **music** may be found in playing an instrument, in singing, in composing, or music appreciation.
- **Art** is a way to express what is beautiful and appealing in a visual way. Painting or drawing is foremost. Crafts such as quilting, sewing, or knitting are part of the Arts.
- **Creativity** is the ability to use one's imagination to see things as they might be. It is the ability to formulate meaningful new ideas or new ways of doing things.
- **Athleticism** is the ability to develop a gift, a skill, or a talent in any athletic sport. Those sports may include individual sports or team sports, such as football, baseball, soccer, track and field, tennis, golf, or bowling; water sports such as swimming, diving, water polo, and boating; or outdoor sports such as backpacking, horseback riding, or bull riding. The list could go on forever. Athleticism may also be the ability to teach and coach others to improve their skills or attain success.

- **Knowledge** is the ability to grasp concepts and master any subject— science, math, geometry, engineering, history, languages, astronomy, computers, etc.

- Some people have a great **memory**. There are those who remember dates, times, events, and places. Others who have a good memory can remember quotes, songs, or words in a book. Still others know where to find things they have seen before—on a shelf, around the house or garage, or just on a pile of papers. Some people have a photographic memory and can see an entire page of a book in their mind.

- **Visual skills** include abilities to visualize space, structure, or dimension. Some people create and build things. Others can envision something different in a space than what currently exists.

Personality characteristics, gifts, and talents have a connection to a person's Color Season and are part of their Divine Colorprint®.

Face Shapes

The shape of your face is part of your Divine Colorprint®. Knowing your face shape, your unique facial features, and the balance that exists between the two is helpful when applying makeup or choosing a flattering hairstyle. The hairline and the jawline are important in determining face shapes for both men and women.

The oval face is considered the ideal shape. The true oval shape is extremely rare. In my experience, every face that is initially thought to be oval is either diamond shaped or oblong.

Round

The cheeks of a round face are as wide as the jaw and the forehead. The hairline is rounded. The chin is full and has no visible jawline.

Square

The square face has a wide forehead with a straight hairline. The forehead, temples, cheekbones, and jaw create an almost straight line down the face. The jaw is prominent and square.

Inverted Triangle

The inverted triangle face has a very broad forehead that is long from the temple to the hairline. The jaw is very narrow.

Rectangle

The rectangular face has very defined angular features. It is longer than it is wide. Prominent cheekbones sometimes make this face shape difficult to determine. Extra weight on the face will cause this shape of face to appear pear or triangular shaped.

Oblong

The oblong face is longer than it is wide. The hairline and the jawline are both slightly rounded.

Diamond

The diamond face is narrow at the forehead and at the chin. The cheekbones are wide.

Heart

The heart shaped face is wide at the forehead and at the cheekbones and narrow at the chin.

Caring for your Skin

Understanding and taking care of your skin is of utmost importance. One of the most important things you can do to ensure you look your best is to have clear, healthy-looking skin. This goes for both men and women. Men especially should take proper care of their skin because they do not usually have the benefit of makeup to hide any flaws. Makeup can do wonders in enhancing beauty potential, but there is a limit as to what can be hidden. A twice-daily skin-care routine that includes cleansing, toning, and moisturizing is essential in producing and maintaining healthy skin.

Regular facial **cleansing** removes dirt, impurities, excess oils, pollution, dead skin, and makeup from the surface of the skin that would otherwise block the pores and create blemishes or cause dry, rough, or aged skin. Moisturizers, serums, and specialized products only work on clean skin.

Face toners prepare the skin for moisturizers and serums while getting rid of excess oil and stubborn dirt or makeup leftover on your face after cleansing.

Moisturizers create and maintain proper levels of hydration that last throughout the day but must be replaced at night. For daytime, SPF 15 is needed and may be supplied by either a moisturizer or a foundation. Nighttime moisturizers are formulated to provide additional emollients. Moisturizers keep the skin looking youthful, soft, and supple. They prevent the skin from becoming dehydrated and looking rough, dull, dry, flaky, wrinkled, and aged. Moisturizers allow for the flawless application of foundation.

Your skin type is part of your Divine Colorprint®. There are four different skin types.

Skin Types

Uniform Skin

This type of skin has a youthful, fresh appearance. The skin is smooth and generally blemish free. Dimples and freckles may or may not be present. There is no such thing as a T-zone where one part of the face is oily and one part is dry for this type of skin. The whole face is always the same. It is either oily all over or it is dry all over. It is uniform.

Pore sizes are medium. Special care must be taken to control oil, reduce surface bacteria, refine pores, and hydrate dry spots. A masque used regularly will be very helpful in keeping this type of skin youthful. People with this skin will also benefit greatly from cleansing both morning and night and by using moisturizer generously. It is important to use an eye treatment product to diminish fine lines and wrinkles around the eyes that will inevitably come with this type of skin.

Sensitive Skin

Sensitive skin is soft and supple and appears to drape over the bone structure. This type tends to have very few wrinkles. Puffiness around the eyes is common. Care must be taken not to stretch the delicate skin under the eyes. Once it is pulled, there is no way to tighten that skin again as there are no oil glands in that area.

Pore size is medium but tends to enlarge as the skin grows more mature. Extra hydration and adequate moisturizer are needed to prevent this type of skin from from developing very fine wrinkles. This skin type will sunburn rather than tan. Windburn, rosacea, and reactions to some skin care products can be expected for those with sensitive skin.

Textured Skin

This skin type may have a rugged appearance and have tendencies to appear leathery or rough. The texture is uneven and may have deep wrinkles and creases—especially as the skin ages. Irregular pigments, sunspots, and age spots are also common.

Pore size is medium to large. Breakouts are deeper in the skin and acne is a problem. This skin is generally a combination of some dryness with oiliness in the T-zone. The support of products that are deep pore cleansing and that can repair damaged skin are beneficial. SPF moisturizers and foundation are critical to protect from sun damage and photo ageing.

This skin type needs rich, emollient moisturizers because the skin lacks elasticity and essential moisture, which makes the lines and wrinkles more apparent. Products that restore moisture, replenish skin nutrients, and generate cell turnover will produce healthier, younger-looking skin. Eye treatments that smooth and tighten the more textured but still tender area around the eye are also important.

Translucent Skin

Translucent skin has a porcelain or reflective quality to it. The skin appears transparent and luminous. Most of the advertisements for skin products use models with this naturally flawless skin.

The challenge of this type of skin is the tendency to be very dry. It is crucial for the proper balance of moisture and oil to be present at every age and stage of life for all the skin types but especially for those with translucent skin.

When this type of skin becomes too dry, it will appear oily as it overcompensates for the lack of moisture by creating an imbalance in the natural acid mantel of the skin.

Moisturizers that are rich in emollients are an essential for translucent skin. Products specifically formulated for the eye area should be used daily, beginning as young as possible. It is common for this skin type to have dark circles under their eyes, particularly as they get older.

Guide to Skin Care

In your twenties, skin cells turn over approximately every twenty days, supplying you with fresh, smooth skin on a regular basis. Since this process slows with age, the need to use products that gently exfoliate as well as cleanse your skin will become increasingly more important in order to maintain healthy, youthful looking skin.

The skin is protein plus water, oil, vitamins, and minerals. It is the largest organ of the body. Healthy skin must be properly fed. However, the skin is the last organ to receive support after food has been processed by the digestive system. All too often, the skin is poorly nourished because of inadequate nutritional intake.

The skin is a key detoxification organ in the body and must be allowed to breathe. If creams, lotions, and cosmetics contain substances that reduce its ability to breathe, this causes the body to retain toxins. Skin that cannot breathe properly experiences many problems: acne, dryness, and accelerated aging.

The skin acts like a sponge. Anything applied on your skin can be absorbed into the bloodstream in approximately 90 seconds. That includes skin care and personal care products, cosmetics and household cleaners—anything that touches your skin. Read labels carefully and choose safe, chemical free, and toxin free products whenever possible.

In addition to your skin type, your skin's condition, your environment, the climate, and your age will determine the skin care system that best suits your needs.

Gather the products of your choice and place those items convenient to where they will be used—usually by the sink or in the shower. When all your products are easily accessible, following your regimen will be quick and easy. It is helpful to line the products up in the order they will be used and return them to their proper place afterwards.

Skin Care Procedure

Touching Your Face

Care should be taken when touching your face. Since ring fingers have little strength, it is best to use them when you are touching your face. Use small circular motions, always moving in, upward, and outward from the center of your face to your hairline.

There are no oil glands around the eyes. Pat gently under the eye, moving from the side of your face to the middle of your nose. This will prevent pulling too hard under the area where bags usually appear. Pulling too hard or rubbing your eyes in this delicate area will create puffy bags under your eyes, which are impossible to remove.

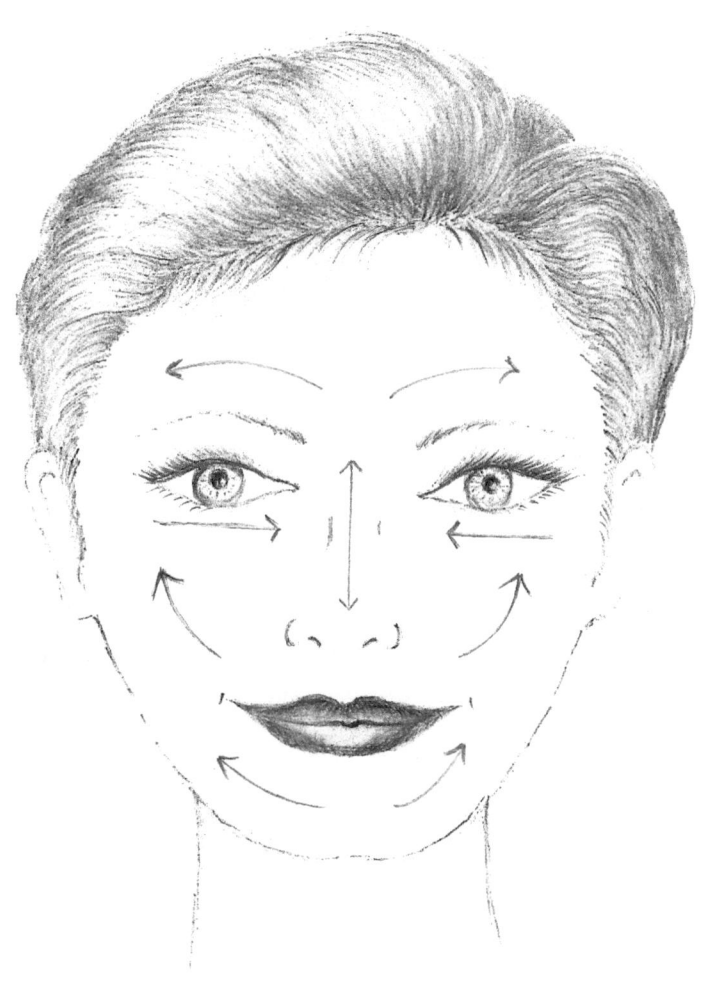

Step 1: Remove Eye Makeup

Use cotton balls or cosmetic pads that are 100% cotton. Synthetic materials will scratch your delicate skin.

Move from the outside of the eye toward the nose as you work in this area of the face. Do not pull! There are no oil glands around the eye area. If you consistently rub and pull, soon you will have bags around and under your eyes that will never go away.

- Gently dot one eye with a cotton ball moistened with eye makeup remover. Give the product a chance to do its work by letting it sit for a minute.
- During this time, go to the next eye. Moisten with eye makeup remover.
- Return to the first eye and gently remove all traces of eye shadow and mascara.
- Do the same with the second eye.*

* Eye makeup left on through the night will become an irritant while you are sleeping and may cause red eyes and red-rimmed eyes in the morning.

Step 2: Cleanse and Exfoliate

The first and most important step of any skin care regimen is proper cleansing and exfoliation.

- Moisten your face and neck with water. The water activates the ingredients in the cleanser. Include the entire area you would see in a portrait, so that you do not potentially end up with a young face and an old neck.

- Gently massage cleanser over the entire face & neck area.

- Rinse thoroughly and pat dry with a soft washcloth or towel.

Step 3: Tone and Soothe*

Toner is essential to preserve youthful skin. This step is very important and should not be overlooked.

Toner refines the pores to keep them small, brightens the skin, and improves the skin's ability to receive and retain moisture.

- Saturate a cotton ball with toner and gently smooth over both your face and neck.
- Do not add water to the cotton ball.
- Wait until skin is dry before proceeding.*

*If acne is a problem, apply an acne treatment that will reduce oiliness, clear up existing blemishes, prevent new blemishes, unclog the pores and speed healing. Proceed as follows.

Step 4: Moisterize and Replenish

The lack of moisture and oil is a major cause for dry skin and for wrinkled skin.

- Gently pat an eye cream or eye treatment around the eyes.

- Apply any serums and specialized creams.

- Apply a daytime moisturizer evenly over the face in the morning and a nighttime moisturizer in the evening.*

- Soften, smooth, and protect your lips with lip balm or lip conditioner.

* When moisturizing, remember your hands and feet so they too remain soft and supple. Feet do not become clean by merely standing in the shower. Scrub them with soap and water, dry, and apply lotion or cream.

Step 5: Purify and Renew

A mask stimulates natural cell renewal, draws out surface impurities, tightens your skin, keeps pores small, and increases smoothness of your skin.

- Once or twice a week, spread a generous amount of masque on your face and neck.
- Avoid getting too close to your eyes and your lips. You should look like a raccoon when you have the masque on your face.
- Let set for 10 to 20 minutes. You should feel the masque draw and tighten. It should be dry before you remove it with water.
- Splash water all over your face until it loosens the masque.
- Rinse thoroughly.
- Pat dry.

The Art of Makup

Wearing makeup in your seasonal colors enhances individual beauty. Every woman benefits from wearing makeup. Makeup instantly makes you feel good about yourself and lifts your mood. You will carry those feelings with you and be prepared for whatever the day may bring. Life is full of unexpected events. Coco Channel said, "I don't know how a woman can leave the house without fixing herself up a little—if only out of politeness. And then, you never know, maybe that's the day she has a date with destiny. And it's best to be as pretty as possible for destiny."

Think of makeup as an accessory—a very important one. Makeup makes a person more noticeable. It presents you as being someone with enough self-esteem to presume you are worthy of attention.

Authentic, natural beauty is revealed with the artful application of makeup. When the colors of makeup are right for you and are applied correctly, you gain confidence in your appearance. You know you look your best. A sense of self-assurance and self-confidence is created and communicated to others. They will sense that and perceive you as being smart, capable, talented, and trustworthy.

The Spring Seasons usually choose makeup colors that are light and colorful. The Summers prefer a soft, translucent look. Autumns will like either a spicy-and-rich or muted-and-subtle appearance. Winters are naturally drawn to colors that are dark or clear, bright, and dramatic.

When it is time to apply makeup, it is helpful to have a place where the mirrors and lighting allow you to see your whole face up close without showing any shadows. Color cosmetics, brushes, and supplies in appropriate containers that are conveniently placed will simplify any routine. A dressing table is an ideal makeup space. You can also stand in front of the bathroom mirror and have a hand mirror to use up close. Another option is to pull out the top drawer in your bathroom vanity, pull up a chair to the drawer, and use the drawer as a place to set your mirror and hold your supplies.

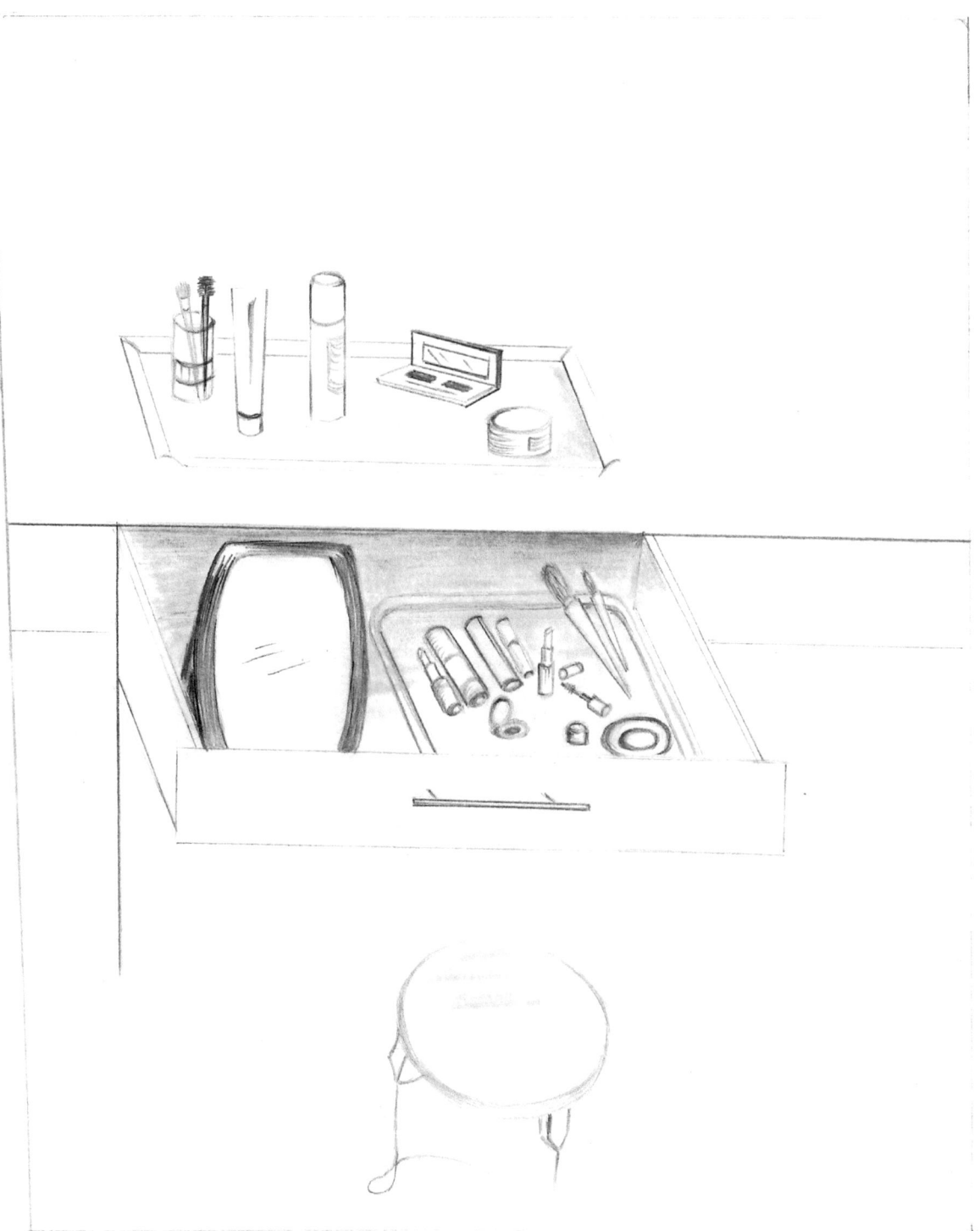

Makeup Brushes are the Artists Tools.

Makeup application is an art. Think of your face as an artist's canvas. Makeup brushes are necessary for creating the proper effects. Some brushes are specifically designed for the application of powders, while others are for applying concealer, foundation, and lipstick. Purchase what is appropriate for each task.

- Concealer brush: firm and tapered at the end—for use around eyes and T-zone
- Foundation brush: a large version of the concealer brush used for a smooth sheer effect—foam sponges can be used as an alternative
- Powder brush: large fluffy brush—use only for powder
- Blush brush: accentuates your cheekbones with blush or bronzer
- Eyeshadow all-over brush: used for the primer shadow
- Two or three contour brushes: one or two for the lid and one for the crease of the eye
- Angled eyeliner brush: used to apply accent under eyeliner, eyebrow color, etc.
- Brow brush: brush up your brows.
- Eyelash curler
- Eyelash comb: separate your eyelashes
- Lip brush: small, firm, narrow tapered brush for greater control in lipstick application

Wash makeup brushes once a week. Washing them preserves the hair and shape. Special products are available or regular shampoo can be used. When using shampoo, rinse thoroughly.

Cosmetics in your Seasonal Colors are the artist's palette.

- Concealer
- One to two shades of mineral powder foundation, lightweight liquid foundation, or Beauty Balm to match your skin tone
- Blush
- Mineral setting powder
- Eyeliner
- Three or more eyeshadows
- Mascara
- Lip gloss
- Lip liner pencils: pencils are usually dryer than lipstick for staying power
- Two to three lipstick colors

Q-tips, a sharpener for cosmetic pencils, cosmetic paddles, a brush holder, and an organizer of some sort for your supplies will be helpful.

General Guidelines for the Artful Application of Makeup*

*These suggestions do not include contouring or corrective techniques.

Step 1: Concealer:

- Hide dark circles under your eyes.
- Remove darkness between the bridge of the nose and the inside corner of the eye.
- Cover the redness in the cheeks.
- Camouflage any blemishes.
- Hide any discolorations on your face.
- Minimize the darkness in the crease around the nostrils and down to the mouth.
- Fill in the lines—particularly around the mouth area.

Procedure:

1. Using a small concealer brush, begin at the inner corner of the eye well and work outward.
2. Blend carefully by touching and pressing with a sponge or your fingertips, being careful to keep the concealer on the dark areas only.
3. Do not pull. Always work with a light touch and with a pat and roll motion—to avoid giving gravity a helping hand. The objective is to always add lift to the face.
4. Wipe off the brush and your fingers on a tissue between applications.
5. Apply to other areas as needed.

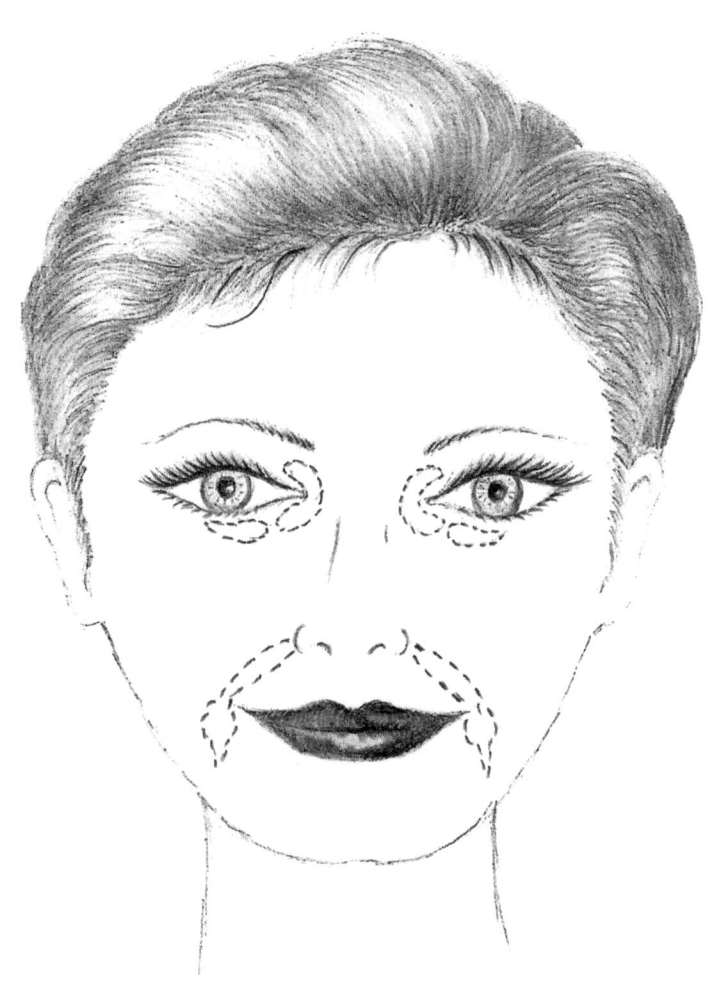

Step 2: Foundation

- Even out your skin tones—do not create a mask.

- Enhance the texture of your skin.

- Minimize complexion flaws and blemishes.

- Moisturize and protect against UV damage and environmental pollutants.

Wearing foundation in your seasonal shade should be considered part of a skin care regimen even if you wear no other makeup.

Procedure: Apply immediately after cleansing, toning, and moisturizing.

1. Shake liquid foundation well before using.

2. When using either a liquid or a cream foundation, put a small amount of foundation on the side of one hand between the pointer finger and the thumb. Use this surface like an artist's palette. If you need to mix colors to get the right shade, add a drop of the secondary color, then mix the two colors together on your hand before applying to the face.

3. Dip brush into foundation and apply evenly over your entire face, starting in the center of your face and moving outward and upward.

Step 3: Blush

- Give your face dimension.
- Contour and define your cheekbones.
- Emphasize and brighten your eyes.

Procedure:

1. Dust a small amount of powder blush on your brush.
2. Tap off the excess.
3. Brush high on the cheekbones to give lift to the face and emphasize the good points of your bone structure. Your cheeks should look as if they were touched by the sun. Apply color no lower than the nose and no closer than the iris of the eye.
4. Blend so there are no visible lines of demarcation.

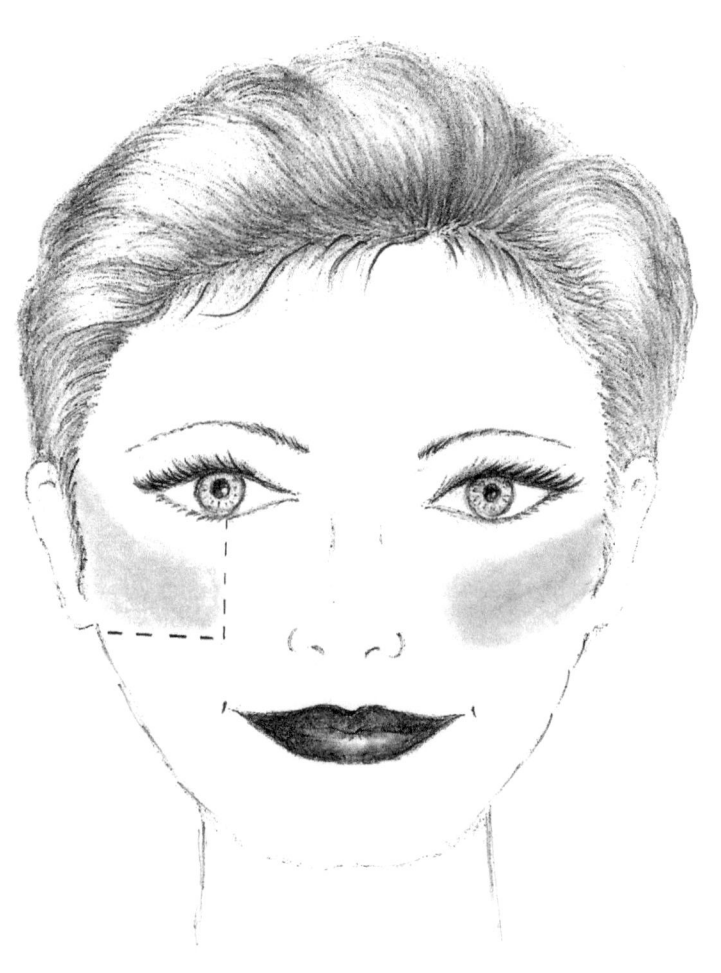

Step 4: Powder

- Set your foundation and concealer to last longer.
- Give your face a finished look.
- Add velvety softness to the skin.
- Obscure fine lines and wrinkles.
- Press onto the eyelids with a wedge before applying liner and shadow to allow eye makeup to sit better and last longer.
- Use as the ultimate touchup.

Procedure:

1. Choose a mineral powder that closely matches your foundation.
2. Using only the tips of the powder brush, pick up a small amount of powder.
3. Shake off the excess by tapping against your hand.
4. Dust on your face in light strokes—outward across the forehead and under the eyes and downward on the rest of the face. This is the one time that you use a downward stroke on the face. There are very small hairs on your face. If you brush upward, they will show.

Translucent powder brushed across the jaw line will give lift to the face—applied on the cheekbone immediately under the eye will highlight your eyes.

Bronzing powder imitates the healthy look of sun and adds color all over the face. Dust lightly over the apples of the cheeks, nose, and chin. When used under the chin, it will make your neck recede.

Step 5: Eyebrows

Eyebrows are the frame for your eyes and an accent for your face.

The natural shape of your brow as a child should be followed as an adult. That natural brow shape complements, enhances, and emphasizes the shape, color, and proportion of your eyes. Eyebrows do not always grow back once they are removed, so plan carefully.

Upward

Straight

"S" Shape

Curved

High Arch

Soft Arch

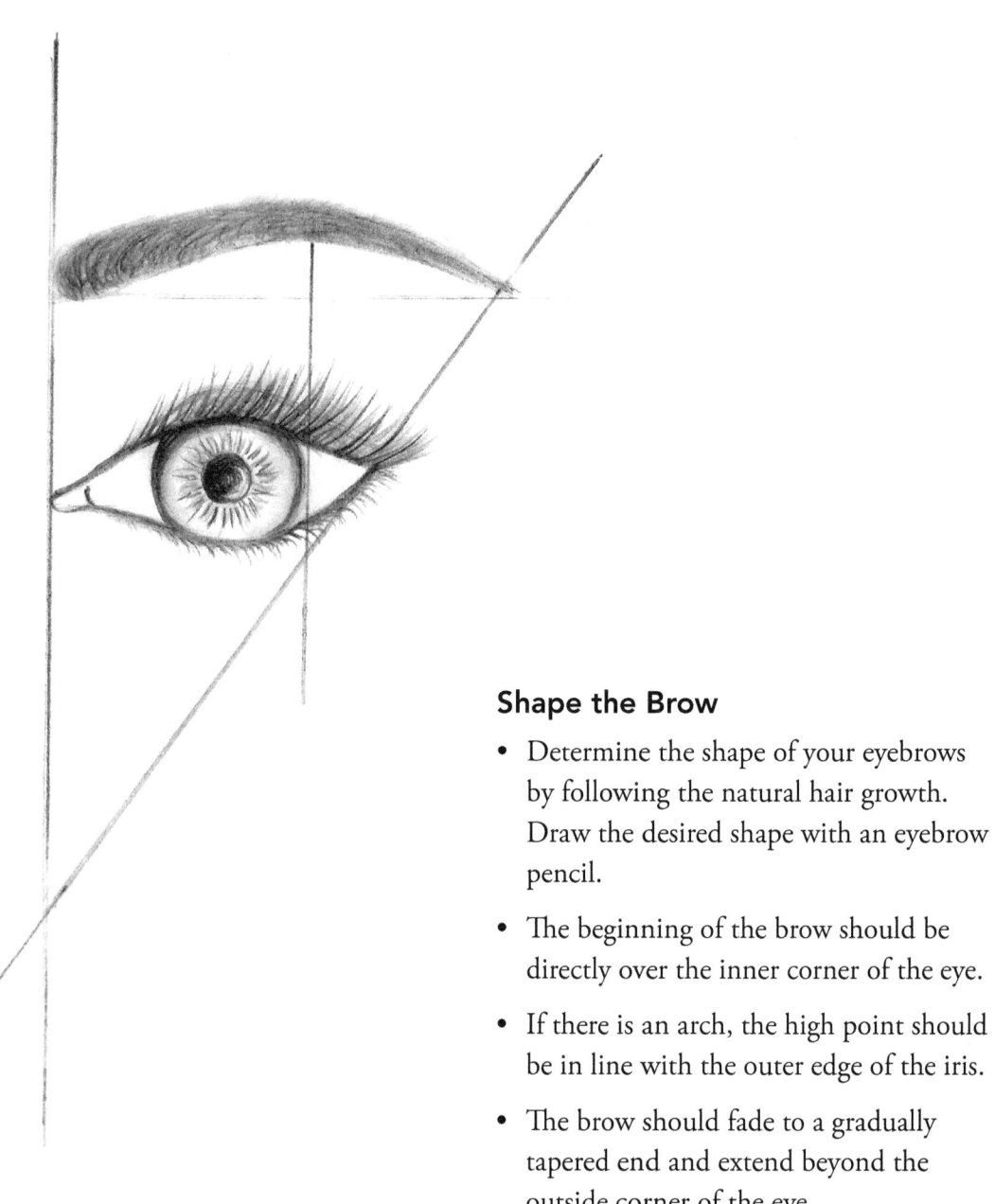

Shape the Brow

- Determine the shape of your eyebrows by following the natural hair growth. Draw the desired shape with an eyebrow pencil.

- The beginning of the brow should be directly over the inner corner of the eye.

- If there is an arch, the high point should be in line with the outer edge of the iris.

- The brow should fade to a gradually tapered end and extend beyond the outside corner of the eye.

Rules for Tweezing

1. Invest in a good pair of tweezers.
2. The best time to tweeze is following a shower or bath. Otherwise, run hot water into a sink and lean your face over the water so you feel the steam on your face for a few minutes.
3. Apply a rich moisturizing cream to your brow.
4. Tweeze the brows in the direction of hair growth, removing any eyebrow hairs that grow outside the desired curve and between your eyes.
5. Grasp one hair at a time pulling in a very quick motion.
6. Work from the inner corner to the outer end and from the bottom to the top.
7. Work one line at a time, and analyze your brow before proceeding. When it looks the way you want, quit.
8. Follow tweezing with a calming lotion or moisturizer.

Fill in Your Brows with Color

- Choose the color that matches your brow as it appears naturally.
- For some, the color of their eyebrows will be close to their hair color. Others will have hair of one color and brows of another.
- Redheads who do not have red eyebrows will find that blond or a shade of camel brown will work best.
- Those with black hair will find that dark grey or the darkest brown is the best choice.
- Typically, brows should be one shade darker than your hair, if your hair is light, and one shade lighter than your hair, if your hair is dark.

Procedure:

1. With a very sharp pencil or eyebrow applicator brush, use short light strokes to fill in the brow to the desired shape.
2. Brush eyebrows upward to lift the face.
3. Set with an eyebrow gel or wax.

Step 6: Eye Shadow

- Emphasize the focal point of your face.
- Intensify the color and size of your eye.
- Create a sense of drama. Smoky eyes are complimentary to the seasons who wear the darker colors. They are too intense for the lighter or muted seasons.

There are seven different eye shapes:

1. **Balanced**: eyes are evenly set on the face
2. **Hooded**: lids and crease are not visible when the eye is open
3. **Prominent**: eyes are forward in the eye sockets
4. **Deep Set**: eyes are set back into the eye sockets
5. **Close Set**: eyes are both close to the bridge of the nose
6. **Wide Set**: width between the eyes is noticeable
7. **Mono-lid**: eyes have no defined crease

Lighten areas you want to bring forward, enhance, or make appear larger. Darken areas you want to recede, minimize, or subdue. The basic rules for eye shadow application suggest a medium tone on the eyelid, a dark hue in the crease to add depth to the eyes, and a paler shade under the brow for highlighting. There are exceptions to this rule.

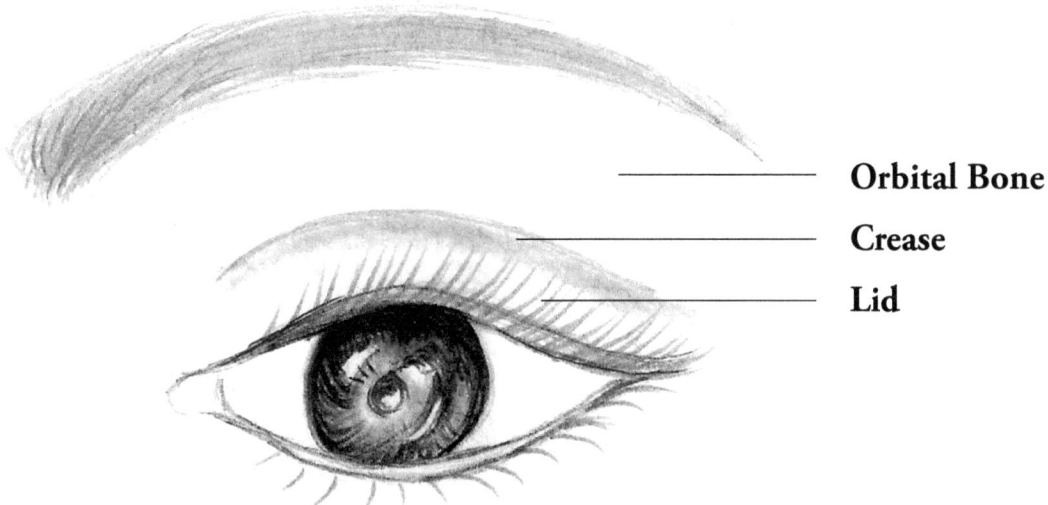

Use the appropriate eye shadow brush in each step of application.

1. Cover the entire eye area from lashes to eyebrows with primer, concealer, or foundation.

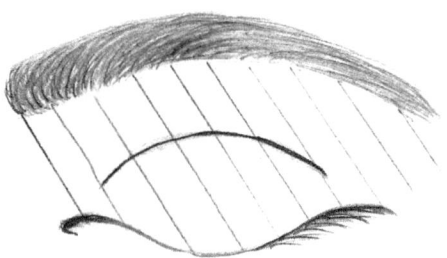

2. Apply a neutral or nude shade of eyeshadow over the entire eye area. Swipe your brush across the eye shadow. Tap your brush to remove the excess eye shadow from the brush before applying the eyeshadow.

3. Using the same technique, apply the lid color of your choice about three quarters of the way up with a contour brush. This color is usually a clear, bright light to medium shade. If you have redness around your eyes, do not use shadows with a pigment.

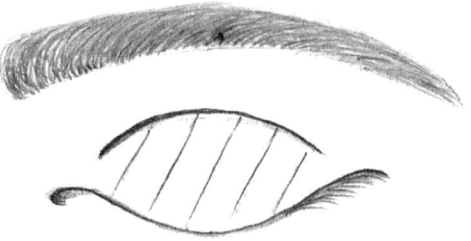

4. Working from the outside toward the center, apply a second color of shadow on the orbital bone and in the crease using a rounded or angled eyeshadow brush. Form a triangle at the outer edge of your eye. This color should be darker than the first shadow.

5. If you want more definition, draw a thin line in the crease of your eye with a dark color from your palette. Use an angled eyeliner brush with stiff bristles for control.

6. Use a very light shadow to accentuate the area just under the outer eyebrow.

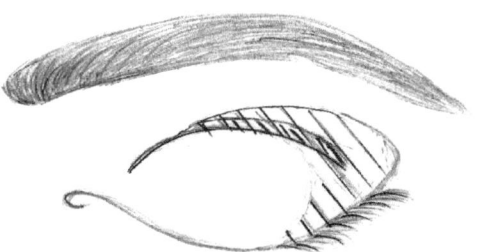

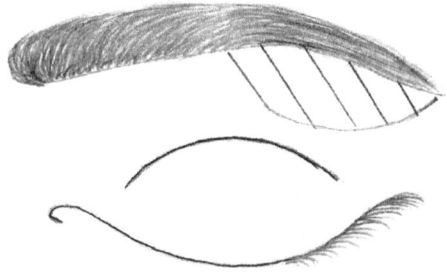

7. To accentuate the eyes, make a thin line with the same light shadow you used under the outer brow under the liner on your lower lid using an angled eye liner brush.

Step 7: Eyeliner

Eyeliner defines your eyes and makes them appear larger and more pronounced.

1. Apply liner as close to the lash line as possible with a sharp pencil or liquid eyeliner.
2. On the top lid, begin at the inner corner of the eye with a very thin line. As you move to the outer corner, the line should become slightly thicker. This procedure "lifts" the eye and emphasizes the eye's shape.
3. Extend the line beyond your natural eye with a slight upward stroke.
4. Line the bottom lid, beginning where the lashes grow. Draw a thin line that connects to the line you have drawn for the upper lid. Your eye will look larger using this technique.
5. Leave the lines defined or smudge softly with a Q-tip or a brush.

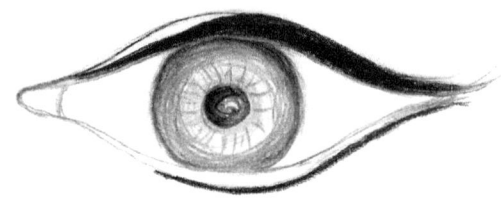

Step 8: Curl Your Eyelashes*

*Curling your eyelashes makes your eyes appear larger.

1. Place the eyelash curler close to the base of the lashes.
2. Squeeze the eyelash curler.
3. Raise the eyelash curler to a horizontal position.
4. Hold for several seconds.

Step 9: Mascara

1. Twist the mascara wand as you slowly pull the wand from the holder. Pumping the wand in the tube will dry out the mascara.
2. Apply mascara to the tops of the upper lashes.
3. Tilt your head back. Coat the upper lashes from base to tip moving from side to side as you move upward. Wait a few minutes for the mascara to dry.
4. A second coat of mascara will make your lashes look thicker.
5. Separate the lashes by brushing with an eyelash separator comb.
6. For the bottom lashes, tilt your head down. Brush across the lower lashes.
7. Using the length of the brush, separate the lower lashes.

Note: For sanitary reasons, replace your mascara every three months.

Eyelash extensions are another option. Extensions that are too long and too thick will hide rather than enhance the eye.

Step 10: Lip Liner and Lipstick

- Provide necessary moisture to prevent dry lips
- Improve the shape of your lips
- Hide little imperfections
- More staying power
- Prevent lipstick from feathering into lines that may be around the mouth

Lipliner can match the lipstick closely or be a darker shade to add some contrast. Purchasing three different lipsticks provides a lot of versatility in your color selection. Use each alone, mix and match any two colors, or layer three to create many variations.

1. With lip liner in hand, rest your little finger on the chin for support.
2. Line the upper lip working from each corner to the center of your lip. The higher point of the curve should be directly under the center of each nostril.
   - To make a lip appear fuller, line outside your natural lip line and very slightly round out the top edges.
   - To make the upper lip appear smaller, line inside the natural lip line.
   - Even out any irregularities with the lip pencil.
3. Line the lower lip in one movement from one side to the other. If the lower lip is fuller than the upper lip, line inside the lip line. If the lower lip is smaller, draw outside the lip line.
4. Apply lipstick from the tube or with a lip brush. Blot lightly.
5. Layer with additional colors, blotting between each application.
6. Highlight the center of the lip with a lighter shade. Lipstick is more moisturizing than gloss.
7. Apply lip gloss.
8. Blot with a tissue to prevent teeth from getting smudged.

Nail Care

Well-manicured nails are the finishing touch. This is true for both men and women.

1. Nails should be neatly trimmed or filed following the natural shape of your fingers.

2. Cuticles should be pushed back into the nail bed.

3. Polish, when used, can be clear, a vibrant hue, or a neutral shade from your color palette.

Hair Fashion

Your hair is one of the first things others notice about you. It is the frame for your face. The hairstyle you choose should flatter the shape of your face. Your hair has certain properties that cannot be changed. Your hair is either thin or thick. It is fine or coarse. It is straight, wavy, or curly.

Straight hair usually has a natural sheen to it. It is difficult to curl and will not hold curl well. Frizzy hair is a variation of wavy hair. Both are resistant to styling. Everyone who has wavy hair has a definite shape to their wave. Natural curls may be soft and flowing, or they may be tight and springy.

The most flattering styles for any individual are those that follow their distinct pattern and suit their Season and their personality. A style that works for one person—even though it is popular—will not look good on others.

The importance of a good haircut cannot be overemphasized. Some styles require a blunt cut. Other styles need a layered cut to look their best.

Animated and Lively Hairstyle

Some hairstyles are animated and lively. These styles often have an upward or buoyant movement. The hair should appear wispy, airy, or pieced. Pixie cuts and layered cuts fit this description. To achieve this look, hair should not hang below the jawline. Hair that is worn to the jawline should be kept close to the crown and flipped upward. Hair on the back of the neck should be kept short.

Soft and Flowing Hairstyle

The soft and flowing style often has soft, curly curls or waves. When worn short, styles that have height in the crown and width at the temples will emphasize the natural flow of the waves or curls.

A soft upsweep worn away from the face works beautifully for this type of hair.

Hair that is pulled back tight away from the face does not look good. A middle part and straight hair should also be avoided.

Casual and Random Hairstyle

Some hair lends itself to styles that are casual and random. This hair type lends itself to asymmetrical, pointy, or broken lines. Irregular, angular cuts where the hair sticks almost straight up, moves in different directions, or lies close to the head all fit this pattern. Tight or unruly curls, which are a characteristic, should be worn full around the face. Ponytails worn high on the head that are sometimes messy follow this pattern. A hairstyle called the shag is casual and edgy and fits this description.

Once again, face-framing hairdos and middle parts should be avoided. Layered cuts work for casual and random styles.

Smooth and Defined Hairstyle

Smooth and defined styles look smooth, even, and sleek. These styles are great for straight hair. Any variation where hair is pulled back away from the face is a great choice. Curls and waves should be exact. Blunt cut styles are characteristic.

Whatever style you choose, proper hair care requires frequent shampooing and conditioning. Hair should be washed often enough to prevent the buildup of oils. Conditioner prevents both your hair and scalp from becoming too dry.

A healthy head of hair also requires proper nourishment. If your diet is inadequate, that will be apparent in the appearance of your hair.

At every age and stage of your life, the natural color of your hair is the most complimentary and flattering color you could possibly choose. Your natural hair color is always in harmony with your season. Whenever you change the natural color of your hair to something totally different, it will also change the way you present yourself to the world. The overall impression of who you truly are inside will be lost.

As you grow from childhood to adulthood, hair color changes naturally. It usually gets darker. This darker shade is the best for you at this time of life. It is your natural pattern within your Divine Colorprint®. It is more common for children with dark hair to retain their dark color than it is for children who were blonde to remain blonde. Whatever the shade, tone, and depth your hair becomes, the natural color of your hair always perfectly complements the undertones in your skin.

There is such a strong feeling in our current culture that gray hair is to be avoided at all costs. Because everyone has been led to believe that gray hair makes one look old, it is difficult to even consider the thought of going gray. It requires a change in mindset to accept the fact that hair in the natural process of turning gray or that is already gray, will actually make you look more youthful than trying to cover the gray with color. Wearing your seasonal colors when your hair is gray makes a significant difference in maintaining a youthful appearance.

There are many variations of gray hair. There are shades of gray that are silver, white, frosty, or crystalline. There are also soft, muted shades of gray. Some grays contain a tint of pale gold or are oyster white. Gray hair may also be an iron gray or pewter with a bit of a green cast. Whatever shade of gray in your hair, women with gray hair will look striking and men will look distinguished. Both will look amazing.

The best choice for those who choose to color their hair and have medium to light hair is to go one or two shades lighter or darker than their natural hair. If hair is dark, always go lighter. Using dark colors—especially black—will be too harsh and severe. The high contrast seasons—Cool Clear Winter, Bright Clear Winter, and Bright Warm Spring—should not use highlights as those highlights will diminish the impact of the natural contrast that exists between the skin and hair.

If blonde is the hair color of choice, the shade of blonde you choose should suit your season. Spring Seasons will look best using variations of golden blonde. The Summer Season blonde is more of an ash shade. Honey blonde is the best shade for Autumn Seasons. Platinum blonde is the best choice for the Winter Seasons.

Conclusion

There is a connection to the patterns of our lives and the colors that suit us best. Color analysis is a life-changing event. The many changes that occur from having an accurate color analysis by a FabYouLook® stylist cannot all be shown simply with "before and after" pictures, such as for a typical makeover. Color analysis is much more deeply involved. Once someone has identified their personal Divine Colorprint® and embraced their personal Season, a beneficial and lasting change occurs that is difficult to explain. This change occurs internally and is reflected outwardly. You will feel confident and secure in your color choices when you know which season of the Twelve Seasons on the Color Continuum you identify with and when you understand what colors are best for your season.

Your countenance will change and your appearance will improve when you know the shape of your face, your skin type, how to care for your skin, how to artfully apply makeup, and how to fashion your hair. Having the correct hair color and wearing correct clothing colors will brighten your appearance. An amazing sense of self-worth and self-assurance comes as a natural result of knowing and embracing your color season and your Divine Colorprint®.

Learning the many ways color can change the way you look, the way you feel, and the way you see yourself is important in the process of becoming the best version of you.

FAB
YOU
LOOK

Visit www.FabYouLook.com
Contact Linda
Schedule a Color Analysis or a Style Analysis
Apply to become a FabYouLook® Stylist